Masako's Story

Surviving the Atomic Bombing of Hiroshima

Revised Second Edition

Kikuko Otake

authorHOUSE®

AuthorHouse™
1663 Liberty Drive
Bloomington, IN 47403
www.authorhouse.com
Phone: 1-800-839-8640

First published by AuthorHouse 12/22/2011

ISBN: 978-1-4634-4336-8 (e)
ISBN: 978-1-4634-4337-5 (hc)
ISBN: 978-1-4634-4338-2 (sc)

Library of Congress Control Number: 2011914162

Printed in the United States of America

To Sverre + Gerd,

Masako's Story: Surviving the Atomic Bombing of Hiroshima

Let there be Peace!

Kikuko

May 10, 2012

To Nobuichi
who died during the atomic bombing of Hiroshima

To Masako
who lived through the bombing and its aftermath

Foreword

We can never say for certain how human beings will respond to the harm inflicted upon them. Some of us may seek vengeance or justice (and sometimes the distinction is less than clear). Others may internalize their trauma and revisit it upon themselves or upon others—a cycle of violence familiar to abusers and their victims. Still others may try to forgive the perpetrator and put the offense behind them. Violence against entire populations can provoke wars, revolutions, or acts of terror.

Sometimes—not often enough—those who have suffered terribly at the hands of others look for higher moral ground. Gold Star Mothers and some veterans returning from Iraq and Afghanistan (and Vietnam before them) have marched to insist that no one else's sons and daughters be killed in pointless wars. Some of the families of those who died in the terror attacks of September 11, 2001 have renounced wars of retaliation that have killed members of other families thousands of miles away. Relatives of murder victims have, on occasion, spoken out passionately and eloquently against the death penalty. While they may forgive, they do not wish to forget, and make it part of their life's work to ensure that the meaning of their loss is not forgotten or misappropriated by the larger community.

Perhaps in no place and at no other time in history has this desire been more manifest than among the hibakusha—the survivors of the US atomic bombings against Hiroshima and Nagasaki. For more than 60 years—since those terrible mornings in August 1945 when the lives of more than 100,000 people were snuffed out instantly in two fireballs brighter than the sun—the hibakusha have told their personal stories and have shared the pictures of their burned and broken bodies, not to evoke pity or to extract apologies, but to move the rest of us to a determination that no one else will ever suffer in this way. "No more Hiroshima! No more Nagasaki!" is the appeal of all hibakusha, reiterated here in the story of Kikuko Otake's mother, Masako.

One can visit the peace museums in Hiroshima and Nagasaki—as I was privileged to do a few years ago—and learn the history of the bombings from hundreds of photos and descriptions. Seeing the twisted wreckage of the A-bomb dome for the first time is a shock for which photos and film clips cannot prepare you. Yet none of these artifacts conveys the abhorrent nature of nuclear weapons as well as words from a survivor:

> "Fallout sticks to my bone marrow, and keeps on releasing
>   radiation,
> Radiation that will continue to eat away at me,
> Even after my death."

By presenting her mother's story (and her own) as a series of prose poems, Kikuko Otake has opened up possibilities for narrative expression more typical of song. I was reminded of a poem by Nazim Hikmet, set to music and recorded by the American folk-rock band the Byrds, which haunted me throughout much of 1966 and helped push me towards a life as a peace activist:

> I come and stand at every door
> But no one hears my silent prayer
> I knock and yet remain unseen
> For I am dead, for I am dead.
>
> I'm only seven though I died
> In Hiroshima long ago
> I'm seven now, as I was then
> When children die they do not grow.
>
> ...All that I ask is that for peace
> You fight today, you fight today
> So that the children of this world
> May live and grow and laugh and play.

The moral education at the heart of hibakusha narratives supports a call to political action. Hiroshima and Nagasaki survivors, knowing from their own experience that nuclear weapons must never be used again, have appealed for their abolition. Mayors for

Peace, led by Hiroshima Mayor Tadatoshi Akiba, have demanded the commencement and successful conclusion of negotiations on a Nuclear Weapons Convention, with the goal of achieving a world free of nuclear weapons by 2020, to ensure that some hibakusha will live to witness the realization of their dream. The mayors have been joined in this call by doctors, scientists, educators, lawyers, parliamentarians... even by some military leaders and former cold warriors who have come to realize that such omnicidal weapons are intolerable.

Readers of *Masako's Story* will find the appeal of the hibakusha reflected on every page of Kikuko Otake's intimate memoir: Hear the stories of those who died and those who survived to bear witness. Take those stories to heart. Remember that as humans we are capable of terrible cruelty and infinite compassion, and embrace the latter. No more Hiroshima! No more Nagasaki!

John Loretz
Program Director, International Physicians for the Prevention of Nuclear War

[IPPNW, the recipient of the 1985 Nobel Peace Prize, launched the International Campaign to Abolish Nuclear Weapons in 2007. For more information, and to get involved in the global campaign for a nuclear-weapons-free world, visit www.ippnw.org and www.icanw.org.]

Acknowledgements

I first wrote about my atomic bomb experiences in my Japanese language book *Amerika e Hiroshima kara (To America from Hiroshima)*, which was published in 2003. Focusing on the text of Chapter One and some poems in Chapter Four from that book, I drafted an English language edition that was published under the title *Masako's Story: Surviving the Atomic Bombing of Hiroshima* from Ahadada Books in 2007. Due to its focus and editing, *Masako's Story* should be considered a separate work and not an exact translation of my original Japanese work.

When the first edition of *Masako's Story* sold out almost completely, I resolved to publish a revised second edition. Wholly new text and poems, as well as additional photographs and illustrations, were inserted.

While preparing the first edition of *Masako's Story*, translating Chapter One was especially difficult because my mother, Masako, related her atomic bomb experiences in Hiroshima regional dialect. When I looked for someone who could bring my mother's unique dialect to English language readers, Professor Hisae Niki, a friend of mine, introduced me to Jesse Glass, Jr., a professor of American Literature at Meikai University in Japan.

Dr. Glass is an award-winning, published poet. He wisely advised me against trying to insert the unique intonations and cadences of Hiroshima dialect into an English language draft. He also suggested that I write the "Letter to the Reader" section that appears in *Masako's Story* and provided additional editorial work. I am so indebted to him. Words alone cannot express how grateful I am for his contributions and wise counsel.

For the revised second edition, my thanks also go out to John Stickler, who is a published poet, novelist and essayist. He has worked tirelessly to find a publisher and to seek grants or endowments for me for more than two years. In the process, we were able to have a foreword written by John Loretz, Program Director of the International Physicians for the Prevention of Nuclear War (IPPNW), a group recipient of the 1985 Nobel Peace Prize. I owe a debt of gratitude to John for the moving foreword that I am so proud to add to the revised edition.

Thanks also go to my youngest son, Bryan Otake. It was Bryan who had the enormous task of preparing the first rough draft of the English language edition and who again went over the entire volume for this revised second edition. He also drew the illustrations that appeared in *Masako's Story*.

Finally, I would like to thank my husband, Hiroshi, and my oldest son, Leo, who were supportive and understanding, especially when I had computer difficulties.

Note: Maps and diagrams on pages 3, 21, 76 and 77 and photographs on pages 20, 28 to 33 and 82 are reprinted with permission of the Hiroshima Peace Memorial Museum. Other pictures and illustrations are the property of the author unless otherwise noted.

Kikuko Otake
August 2011

Contents

Letter to the Reader

Dear Reader:

On August 6, 1945, when the world's first atomic bomb was dropped on Hiroshima, my family lived in the Uchikoshi neighborhood of that city, 1.1 miles north of the hypocenter. It was only a few months before the bombing that my family had moved back to Hiroshima, my parents' hometown, from Nishinomiya near Kobe. It was as if we had returned just so that we could experience the blast. My mother, Masako, was 32 years old. My two brothers, Shoichi and Koji, were 8, and 3 years old, and I, Kikuko, was 5 years old. All four of us barely escaped death, though seriously injured, that day, but my 35-year-old father, Nobuichi Furuta, did not. He had been drafted into the Japanese Army and stationed in Hiroshima. At the time of the bombing, it is likely that he was engaged in morning exercises out in the open on the Western Drill Ground about 550 yards from the hypocenter. He probably died instantly from the extreme flash heat of the atomic bomb, as some reports state that all soldiers were burned to death where they stood in formation. He must have been one of those soldiers. We never found his remains.

I remember almost nothing about the bombing and its aftermath. I find this strange. As I was already 5 years old, I should have been capable of remembering those events. But the atomic bombing was such a horrendous occurrence that even adults could not believe their eyes. Truly, it must have been something beyond the comprehension of my 5-year-old mind.

Masako never talked about those terrible days, even to her children. About two weeks after the bombing, my mother and my two brothers and I fled to Rakuraku-en, a suburb of Hiroshima city, where my grandmother owned some rental houses. We settled and lived in one of them. My mother ended up living in that house for the rest of her life. Our new home stood a mere seven miles away from the hypocenter, but Masako never wanted to take part in the Peace Memorial Ceremony held each year on August 6 in the Peace

Memorial Park near the hypocenter. Similarly, she never visited the Peace Memorial Museum. In simple terms, she refused to see or do anything that reminded her of the bombing. Asking her about the atomic bomb experience had long been a taboo in my family.

I came to the United States in 1968 to marry my Japanese fiancé who was attending graduate school in California. By a strange twist of fate, I ended up becoming a naturalized citizen of the country that had unleashed the atomic bomb on my family and the world.

Because of the time difference between the United States and Japan, the fateful date and time of August 6, 8:15 a.m., the exact moment of the Hiroshima explosion, falls on August 5, 4:15 p.m. in California. Somehow the time difference blunted my emotions at each anniversary. Thus, after coming to the United States, I initially stopped observing the bombing anniversaries. But after a while, I started to think that I should know more about the devastation wrought by the atomic bomb, and that urge grew stronger and stronger as the years went by. What did my mother do on August 6, 1945? Where did my mother, my two brothers and I spend the night of the bombing? How did we survive the ordeal that followed the attack on Hiroshima? I was already over 50 years old when I realized that if I did not ask her about those tragic days, I would never fully know what had happened to me as a child.

Finally, in 1991, I decided to ask Masako to tell her story during my regular summer visit to Japan. About a week into my stay in the family home in Hiroshima, I had an unusually quiet morning, as my two sons had gone out with their cousins, and no relatives or friends were visiting us. Just my mother and I were at home. I gathered up my courage and gingerly asked her to tell me what had happened to us so long ago. Then, to my surprise, Masako did not refuse, and she finally started to talk. So I grabbed a small notebook I kept handy, and jotted down whatever she said.

I think there were two reasons that my mother broke her silence. One was that almost fifty long years had passed since those tragic days. And two, she had developed a need to speak to me, since I had become the child she rarely saw after my going to the United States to marry in 1968.

Masako related her experiences rather calmly in Hiroshima dialect. She clearly recalled all that had happened on August 6 and 7, so she told me about them in detail. But her memory of the precise timing of events or the ensuing days and weeks was foggy. Because of the calamitous nature of events, she must have lost track of the days.

At first, I wanted to know every little detail, so I asked her many questions. How complete was the destruction? Where and how far did she walk the next day while looking for my father? What did she witness along the way? Where did we go? What did we do during the hours and days after the bombing?

While asking Masako these questions, I gradually came to realize how cruel I was acting. I should not make her remember such experiences, I thought. It had taken her almost fifty years for the trauma of her memories to recede. Why was I pressing her to describe that living hell? While jotting down such depressing events, somehow, I started to think that it was enough, that I did not want to know any more.

As one heart-rending image followed another, I lost my will to transcribe what my mother was saying in her quiet voice. My note-taking ended after writing only six pages.

For the next ten years, I did not even review my notes.

But in 2001, I finally gained the courage to delve into my family history again. By this time, Masako had become bed-ridden with advanced Parkinson's disease, and she could not even recognize me. I could not hear about the atomic bomb experience from her any more. Masako passed away on November 30, 2001, from complications of Parkinson's disease.

Based on my mother's account of the atomic bombing, I wrote an autobiographical book of prose poetry, *haiku, tanka* and essays titled, *Amerika e Hiroshima kara (To America from Hiroshima)* in Japanese, and it was published by Maruzen Company, Ltd. in 2003.

Many Japanese friends suggested that I translate my book into English. At first, it seemed like an impossible task. Translating Chapter One was especially difficult because my mother told me her stories about the atomic bomb experience in Hiroshima dialect. How could I transcribe the subtle meanings and intonations of such a distinct Japanese dialect into English? Yet I came to realize that it would be important for the people of the world to know what had happened in Hiroshima on August 6, 1945, and thereafter. So I committed myself to the task of translation.

Masako's Story consists of our family tale of survival in Chapter One as my mother told it and some poems in Chapter Four from my Japanese book. With a non-Japanese readership in mind, footnotes have been added, and some maps, diagrams and pictures inserted into the narrative to aid understanding. I call this book "the English version" because this is not an exact translation of my original Japanese volume. Moreover, I did not attempt to translate Hiroshima dialect, simply because of the wide linguistic gap between English and Japanese when it comes to such matters.

I know that Masako could not fully describe the horrendous events of August 6, 1945 and the days thereafter. They remain beyond human imagination. Like many atomic bomb survivors, I believe that no word, no picture can ever fully communicate the horrors of the atomic bomb.

I would be very happy if this book helps the people of the world to better understand the atomic bomb tragedy, and to think about the consequences of using nuclear weapons. It is comforting to know that many of the American scientists who developed atomic bombs grew to oppose their use against human beings. Nuclear weapons should never be used on human beings under any conditions. Nuclear weapons should be abolished. We should not repeat the evil.

No one else should ever suffer as we did.

As a survivor of the Hiroshima atomic bomb attack, I appeal to the world:

"No more Hiroshima."

"No more Nagasaki."

"No more *Hibakusha*, victims of nuclear weapons."

Nuclear weapons do not destroy only our enemies, but our own humanity, as well as our children's future on planet earth.

Like the physicist and pacifist Ursula Franklin said, "There is no other way of surviving but peace."

Sincerely yours,

Kikuko Otake

P. S. You may not feel comfortable reading this book because of the disturbing text and the horrible pictures. But I would like to remind you that this was what had happened in Hiroshima when the atomic bomb was used against human beings.

Note: To protect the privacy of individuals who appear in this narrative, some names have been changed.

Part I
Masako's Story

My Family

July 1945

From left (age): Kikuko(5), Masako (32), Koji (3) and Shoichi (8)

My father took this picture less than one month before the atomic bomb was dropped. I recall that I did not want to have my picture taken on that day. As I was crying, I had a sad face. Was it because I had a presentiment that something terrible was going to happen?

Flight Path of the *Enola Gay*

August 6, 1945

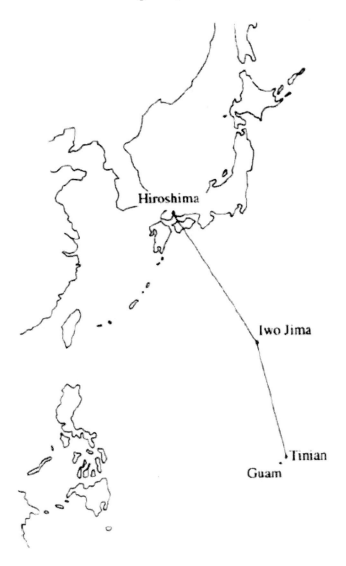

The US B-29 bomber *Enola Gay* departed from Tinian Island near Guam at 1:45 a. m. on August 6 (Japan time). It dropped the atomic bomb over Hiroshima at 8:15 a. m.

1. I Can't Talk About It Today

My dear Daughter.
On that morning,
When I went out to the backyard,
I found a flower blooming on a squash vine
Which the former resident[1] had planted in a small garden in the
    yard.
Oh I tell you, I was so glad!
'Soon we'll have some squash to eat!'
That's what I thought that morning.

Then I saw a lady with a white parasol
Walking beside the railroad tracks.

'It's going to be another hot summer day today,' I thought,
'Best to hurry up and finish the laundry.'

So I went back into the house,
And when I started washing some clothes in the kitchen in a big
wooden tub,
    It was just at that moment,
    WHEN . . .

        The Atomic Bomb fell.

---

1   My family had moved back to Hiroshima, my parents' hometown, from Nishinomiya just
    about a few months before the bombing.

4

The lady flew like a doll from the railroad tracks,
And landed on her back with her parasol still in her hand,
Dead.

Ah, that moment!
Oh, that day!

How horrible it was.

Hell on earth.
. . . .

I don't want to think about it any more.

Sorry, not now.
I can't bring myself to tell you today.

Mushroom Cloud

August 6, 1945

(Approximately one hour after the explosion at 8:15 a. m.)

Illustration by Junko Morimoto Hiroshima Jyogakuin Daigaku

The cloud generated by the explosion rose upward on strong currents of turbulent air. As the pillar of radiation-laden soot and smoke reached the bottom of the stratosphere, it spread horizontally to a diameter of several miles, forming a giant mushroom cap.

2. Oh! I Can't Continue to Speak of It!

I lay unconscious.
How long?
I don't know.
It felt comfortable,
Like taking a nice, long shower.

Gradually . . . a sound filled my ears:
— Children,
— Children screaming,
— Crying for their mother.
I freed myself by pushing off the debris . . .
Our house had collapsed around us . . .
And I discovered that both you and Koji had been buried
Up to your chests in the rubble,
So I crawled across the broken beams and roof tiles,
And I pulled both of you free.

The gashes on your heads . . .
Like a fountain,
The blood spurted down your smudged faces.

I then looked for Shoichi and found him struggling, alone,
To free himself from the wreckage.
He was bleeding from his head and brow.
And oh!
His left eye was smashed.

'What?
Our house?

Our house has been bombed!
A bomb . . . it fell directly on our house![2]
That's what I kept thinking at that time.

I dug through the broken roof tiles, timber, and crumbled stucco
Searching for the emergency bag I kept handy during the war.
I found it!
Then I took out the first-aid kit.
You were bleeding so badly.
I tried to stop the flow
By binding your heads — yours and your brothers' —
With the big triangular cloth bandages.
But the blood still gushed!

The blood clung to your hair
Pasting it to your skulls and streaking your faces,
So that you, daughter, looked like *Oiwa-san*.[3]
The white dress you wore was filthy and tattered,
And dyed ghastly red by the blood.

I searched for more bandages.
But there were no more . . .
I could do nothing . . . but watch my children bleed.

It was then that I noticed,
Flowing down my forehead . . .
Something . . . wet.
I wiped it with my hand . . .
My palm was covered in blood.

---

2   Our house was in Uchikoshi, 1.1 miles north of the hypocenter.
3   A female Japanese ghost with long hair, and a disfigured face streaming with blood.

I was completely unaware until that moment
That the blast of the bomb had shattered the kitchen window;
Fragments of glass had cut the right side of my head, face and
    shoulder.
I bet there was a dozen slivers of glass or more.
I pulled out as many as I could,
Later.

Just under the elbow,
My left arm was ripped open — the gash about four inches long —
Like the inside of a pomegranate.
And through the gash, a bone flashed ivory white.

Fires were breaking out everywhere …
We had to get away.
I stood you three in a row.
"Now hold hands!" I said.
My eight-year-old Shoichi stood on one side, I on the other,
You, my five-year-old daughter, and three-year-old Koji stood in
    between us.
Then I heard our next-door relative, Aunt Kazuko calling,
"Tasukete ! Tasukete kudasai !"[4]

I could only see her hand.
She was buried in debris.
Nobody came to help us.
Fires were burning near,
So I had no time to waste.
I gathered all my strength,
And pulled . . . and pulled . . .

---

4   "Help me! Help me, please!"

Her house was big — two stories tall —
And the thick pillars and stout timbers were like a vise.
To this day, I still don't know how I managed to pull her free
Despite my torn left arm that flapped like a fish.

The Misasa Elementary School, our official neighborhood shelter,
Was already in flames.
So I fled with you to the sandbank on the Yamate River[5] in
    Uchikoshi.

When we arrived at the sandbank,
I was horrified to see
That it was packed with
Grotesquely burned,
Gruesomely wounded,
People.

Some were completely red, with raw flesh burns.
The scorched skin slipped from their bodies,
And hung in loose strips, like paper streamers.
And their faces!
Eyes, noses, mouths, ears had all melted down.
And the hair . . . the hair . . .
Had burned away from the scalps.

A man's arms and legs . . . were almost torn away . . .
We saw his bones protruding like bloody skewers.

And One . . .
Had a gaping hole in his chest . . . his ribs were exposed.

---

5   About 1.25 miles north of the hypocenter. The Yamate River is a tributary of the Ota River.

10

And One . . .
His belly was split open,
And oh, he was holding his bowels in place!

And One . . .
His skull was smashed open . . .
One eye dangled down on his cheek.

And Another . . .
His head was split so badly . . .
I couldn't tell which side his face was on.

All were streaked with blood and dirt.
The lucky ones still wore shreds of pants,
Scorched and tattered though they were.
But most wore no clothes at all.
Their garments were shorn away
Or burned off by the bomb's searing blast.[6]

I saw masses of naked, bloodied, burned flesh, gasping faces so
    disfigured
That I could not tell the men from the women.
This one . . . that one . . .
I had never seen such horror!
Were they truly human beings?

I once saw a painting of hell.
But I swear this sight was more nightmarish than that.

---

6   The blast force was 440 meters per second or 1,000 miles per hour. In the vicinity of the
     hypocenter, the surface temperature reached over 7,000 degrees Fahrenheit. Within 1.25
     miles radius of the hypocenter, most combustible materials, including people's hair and
     clothing, spontaneously ignited if they were exposed to the direct heat rays of the bomb.

Your Dad's oldest brother, Uncle Koichi, had fled
To the sandbank, where we were . . .
I saw that his entire body was scalded . . .
He was dressed in what I thought was shredded cloth,
But which turned out to be strips of his own flayed skin.
His chest was a garden of burned flesh.
The skin from his cheeks and chin hung down,
A shredded mask instead of a face.
His eyes were barely open.
And the raw flesh of his nose had fused with his swollen upper lip,
Which had peeled back to expose his teeth.
He was burned bald.
He held his hands out in front of him, like a ghost.
And from each tip of each finger,
The skin hung down in glove-like pieces.
I asked him, "You are Koichi, right?"
He nodded,
And then knelt and died.

The day turned as dark as night.
I had no idea what time it was.

But even with those dreadful injuries and burns, no disorder
    reigned.
The crowd moved in a strange silence.
Everyone was dazed, in shock,
And lay, crouched, or stood, like ghosts on that sandbank.

Because your clothing was shredded, dirty and bloody,
You needed new things to wear.
But our house was already in flames,

And I couldn't go back for more clothes.

So, after taking off my *monpe* [7] top,

And draping it over you and your two brothers,

I decided I'd go to Aunt Harada's house in Yamamoto [8]

To get some spare garments that were stored there.

Leaving you and your brothers on the sandbank,

I set out alone on foot.

On the way to Yamamoto,

I walked with hundreds of men, women and children who were
    maimed and badly burned.

The burned ones looked just like Uncle Koichi.

Their faces were red or purple and swollen,

And they held their arms up in front of them, [9]

Their skin hanging like tattered cloth.

Some were lucky enough to still have hair,

Though their hair was in a wild nest, covered in dust, and ashen
    from burns.

Hardly anyone was uninjured.

Streaming with blood, with their heads bowed and silent,

They lurched on towards the suburbs,

And away from the threatening flames and black smoke

That wreathed the shattered city.

Here and there, the injured and the burned

Collapsed to the ground,

And dyed the ground dark red with their blood.

---

7   *Monpe* is women's work clothes. The loose-fitting pants are tied at the ankles. During the
    war, *monpe* was women's daily wear.
8   Yamamoto is located about 2 miles north of the sandbank, or roughly 3 miles from the
    hypocenter.
9   Burn victims held their arms up in front of them like ghosts, because lowering their arms
    caused painful throbbing in their fingertips from the blood pooling in each hand.

Those who were walking,
Those who were dead,
They all looked the same:
Ghosts, goblins, and monsters marching to hell.

Thinking back,
I must have looked exactly like they did.

I arrived at Yamamoto and looked for Aunt Harada's house,
But somehow I couldn't find it.

Suddenly I felt a sharp pain in my foot.
"Ouch!"
I must have stepped on a nail or something.
For the first time since the bombing,
I felt the sensation of physical pain.
I was surprised to notice that I had been barefoot all along.
All the roads were scattered with the debris of flattened houses;
Broken roof tiles, shattered glass, nails, timbers, crumbled stucco,
    and huge splinters were everywhere.
Roads were blocked by fallen utility poles and trees,
Charred by the intense flash heat of the bomb.
Power lines hung down overhead, and some lay tangled on the road.

Then my thoughts turned to you three children.
'Would you be able to withstand such horrible sights?'
I berated myself for leaving you alone,
And resolved to go back to you immediately.

But when I came back to the Uchikoshi sandbank,
I was horrified to find that

You children weren't there.
I searched frantically for you.
I was afraid you might have tried to go back home.
But someone said,
"Don't go back home! It's an inferno!"
"Don't go back to search for your kids!"
I felt as if I would go mad
From my frustration and fear.

Then a badly injured lady in her sixties
Who was too weak to flee said,
"I saw three little children crying for their mother:
'Mommy! Mommy!'
They had a *monpe* top over their heads.
The pattern of that top was the same as that on your *monpe* pants.
I wonder if they might be your little ones."
She also added that many evacuees had moved to a nearby bamboo
grove.

So I went to the thicket by the Yamate River that she pointed out
to me,
But could find no sight of you.
Other survivors, however, told me
That a group of people had taken refuge under a bridge
Because of the rain.
That rain is what we now call "black rain,"[10] isn't it?

'Which bridge could it be,' I thought to myself.
'How would I ever find you and your two brothers?'

---

10   About 20 to 30 minutes after the explosion, heavy rain fell on the northwestern areas of
      the city. It was black because the raindrops contained mud and dust stirred up during the
      explosion, as well as soot from the fires. The black rain was highly radioactive.

I panicked.

But then, luckily, I came upon all three of you

Huddled together under the first small bridge I checked.

All of you were crying, *"Okaa-chan! Okaa-chan!"*[11]

Oh. I can't tell you how happy I was to find you!

Thinking back, we were really lucky.

If I hadn't put my *monpe* top over you,

You might have become atomic-bomb orphans.[12]

Under that bridge,

There was also a naked soldier with no cuts or bruises.

But as he was so pale and gray,

His undressed body looked like a marble statue.

I wondered at that, but was forced to leave him.[13]

We slept on the sandbank that night,

Because everywhere we looked,

The city of Hiroshima was a scorched plain

Still smoldering with some flair-ups here and there.

The sandbank seemed like the only safe place.

Our house had burned down,

And we didn't have anything like *futon* quilts with which to cover
    ourselves.

So we pulled up vines of the *yamaimo* yam

---

11   "Mommy! Mommy!"
12   Approximately 2000 to 6500 children lost both parents to the bombing, but the actual number
     is unknown. Source: Audio Guide #11, Hiroshima Peace Memorial Museum.
13   This soldier was likely a burn victim. Burn injuries varied in intensity according to the
     victim's distance from the hypocenter. Burn victims who were directly exposed to the heat
     rays of the bomb within 0.5 mile of ground zero were often charred black and instantly
     killed. Burn victims 0.5 to 1.25 miles from ground zero frequently suffered ghastly, red burn
     wounds, and most of them died within a few days. Those 1.25 to 2 miles from the hypocenter
     often had burn wounds that rendered the flesh grayish white. The fatality rate amongst the
     severely burned was quite high.

That grew on the slope of the river bank,
And covered our bellies with a few strings of them
Just to feel like we had blankets,
Then tried to fall asleep.
With the tattered clothes that were stiff with caked blood,
With the streaks of blood smeared on our dirty black faces,
With the shards of glass still stuck in my face and shoulder,
With my left arm gashed and limp,
All four of us,
Tried to fall asleep on the sandbank of the Yamate River.

It was so cold that night.

The next morning,
Soldiers distributed some rice balls
That had been provided by relief agencies.
During the war, food was so scarce,
And rice balls had become such luxury food.
We hadn't tasted them for months.
Yet you children didn't eat them.
The rice balls had been grilled to prevent them from spoiling.
But looking at the charred rice balls,
You started to wail,
Seeing a reflection of the charred, black skin of so many people
Suffering around us.

Indeed,
A great number of corpses were floating in the river,
And the burned and the maimed lay moaning nearby.

Are they alive?
Are they dead?

A burned woman kept on begging feebly,
"Mizu, Mizu! "[14]
Then suddenly she ceased her calls.
Silent, forevermore.

After seeing so many deaths,
I felt emotionally numb.
I wasn't even sure
If I myself was still among the living or the dead.

But one incident stands out clearly in my mind.
It occurred maybe three days after the bombing
To a woman who, crying over the dead child in her arms,
Found that maggots had hatched on the corpse,
And had started to wriggle in and out of it,
Feasting upon it.
Because she couldn't leave her dead child like that,
She dug a shallow hole in the sand.
And, as there wasn't wood left in the city,
She filled it with some *yamaimo* vines she had pulled up by the roots,
And cremated her child by herself,
Sobbing and wailing as the flames grew higher.

Around Hiroshima,
So many people were cremating their parents and children like that.

---

14   "Water, water!"

The air was filled with the rank, squalid smells of the wounded and
    the unwashed,
With the stench of so many rapidly decomposing bodies,
With the sharp smell of cremated human flesh,
And with the ashen odor of an entire city in ruins.

    Ah, that time on the sandbank.

    I don't know how to describe it all.

    It was truly a living hell on earth.

    Never.

    Oh, never again.
    . . . .

Oh, I can't continue to speak of it!

Fleeing Survivors

August 6, 1945

Diorama at the Hiroshima Peace Memorial Museum

The burn victims held their hands out in front of them, with sloughed off skin hanging from their fingertips like gloves. These survivors were lucky to still have their clothes. But many other survivors were left naked because their clothes had been shorn away or burned off by the bomb's searing blast.

Map of A-bomb Damage

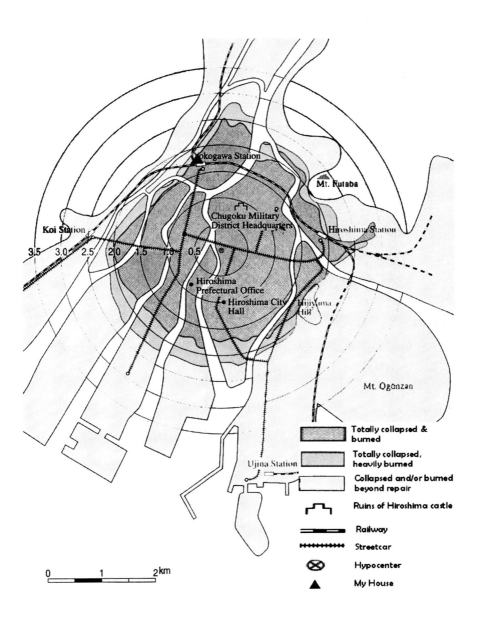

Yokogawa Station

Mt. Futaba

Chugoku Military
District Headquarters

Koi Station

Hiroshima Station

3.5   3.0   2.5   2.0   1.5   1.0   0.5

Hiroshima
Prefectural Office

Hiroshima City
Hall

Hijiyama
Hill

Mt. Ogonzan

Ujina Station

Totally collapsed &
burned

Totally collapsed,
heavily burned

Collapsed and/or burned
beyond repair

Ruins of Hiroshima castle

Railway

Streetcar

Hypocenter

My House

0   1   2 km

21

3. *Nam'amidabutsu*
(May their souls rest in peace)

The morning after the bombing,
I covered you and your brothers with *yamaimo* vines,
And left you on the sandbank to look for your Dad,
A private in the Army's Second Unit of the West,
Stationed very close to the hypocenter.

As far as I could see,
The entire city of Hiroshima had become a scorched plain
That stretched out in all directions.
The roads had mostly disappeared, covered by debris.
Many places were still smoldering,
And the asphalt on the streets was still soft and hot
From the heat of the raging infernos of the day before.
I trudged through block after block of ruined buildings,
Avoiding the dead and the wounded[15]
Who lay scattered everywhere, moaning.

On a wide street,
A packed streetcar during the Monday morning rush hour
Had halted in mid-motion.
Burned and melted . . .
Just a shattered husk . . .
The passengers who had been standing within
Now reduced to charcoal dominos fallen against each other.
Their forms thrust into strange, nightmarish shapes.
Those who had been sitting
Had become blackened, man-shaped lumps of soot of different sizes,

---

15   It is estimated that about 70,000 people died instantly or within a week of the bombing.
Another 70,000 perished by the end of December 1945.

While others had been thrown out of the streetcar,
Their scorched bodies scattered around it.

When I came to the Aioi Bridge,[16]
I stopped in shock:
Its railings were gone,
Fallen into the river.
Though it was made of a foot thick concrete,
A terrible force had lifted the floor girders and sidewalk of that
    great structure.

When I managed to clamber across its twisted spine,
I saw the corpse of a man clinging to a mangled bicycle
Wedged inside the bridge's cracked surface.
He had been scorched to death,
And looked like a crude stick figure made of coal.

The rivers under the bridge were packed with
Thousands of floating corpses and dead horses.[17]
So terribly maimed,
Or burned red, purple, gray or black, and swollen to
Two or three times their normal size,
That I couldn't tell if they were floating on their backs
Or on their stomachs.
But I did notice one dead man bobbing down the river
With his eyes wide open,
Glaring at the sky.

---

16   About 330 yards west of the hypocenter. This T-shaped Aioi Bridge was the target for the
    dropping of the atomic bomb.
17   Horses were used as draft animals by the Imperial Japanese Army.

After crossing the Aioi Bridge,
I walked diagonally across the grounds of the Gokoku Shrine
To take a short cut.
Oh. That ground was filled with hundreds of people with horrible
  burns
Scattered everywhere.
Many of them were dead.
But those that still lived,
Begged, *"Mizu! Mizu o kudasai,"*[18] in faint whispers.
Soon my way was blocked by their outstretched arms.
One of them even grabbed my ankle, though feebly,
To stop me from running past him.
His burned skin sloughed off his fingers,
As I pulled from his grip.

Breathing hard, I found a pipe on the Shrine grounds
That spurted water from its jagged end.
I soaked the bottom half of my *monpe* top with water,
And returned to wring merciful drops onto the lips of the dying.
As their coal-black faces were so gravely disfigured,
Some could not even open their mouths.

The Western Drill Ground where your Dad might have been
Was just beyond these premises.
So I hurried along, chanting, *"Nan'maidabutsu. Nan'maidabutsu."*[19]

But when I came to the Western Drill Ground,[20]
I was told that the soldiers had fled to the Eastern Drill Ground.[21]

---

18 "Water! Let me have a drink of water."
19 Buddhist chant meaning: "May his soul rest in peace."
20 About 550 yards east of the hypocenter.
21 About 1.25 miles east of the hypocenter.

And so I went on ahead, almost as far as Fuchu,[22]
Climbing across the broken span of the bridge
Near Shukkei-en Garden[23] in the process.

All along the way,
I saw thousands of dead bodies scorched by the searing rays of the
    bomb.
Their faces, arms, and bodies were bloated into hideous forms.
Their eyes were swollen shut,
And their swollen lips pulled back into puffed rictus smiles.
They were hairless, and burned so completely,
That their eyebrows had been roasted off,
Making it impossible to tell the bodies of the men from the women.

At one point, I came across a place where many burned soldiers
Had been piled into several heaps.
I looked for your Dad, calling out,
"This is Mrs. Furuta. Is Private Nobuichi Furuta around here?"
The soldiers' stomachs were grotesquely distended,
And looked as if they would burst above and below the belts they
    wore.
They were naked except for their belts and some shoes.
But strangely they retained a small round patch of cropped hair on
    their heads
Where their helmets had kept their hair from roasting off.
As every soldier's face was red and swelled up
Like a balloon because of the severity of their burns,
I could not pick out individual features,
Or tell if one of them was your Dad by looking at their faces.

---

22 The covered distance is about 5 miles.
23 About 0.75 miles from the hypocenter.

When I again said, "Is Private Furuta around here?"
One soldier in the pile opened his eyes slightly,
But closed them right away after realizing his mistake.

Still, you see, by 1945,
Even the military lacked supplies,
And the soldiers had to provide their own belts.
So I tried to find your Dad by searching for his belt,
Using it as a means of identification, if you will.
I prodded one dead soldier on top of the pile a little,
And watched as he rolled down to the foot of the pile.
"I'm very sorry. *Nan'maidabutsu*," I said.
And continued to prod soldiers' bodies,
One after the other, checking each belt in the process.
But soon I started to feel guilty and halted,
Since, although many were dead,
I noticed that others were still dying,
And I was disturbing their last moments.

Pile after pile, there were so many dead soldiers.
I felt powerless to find your Dad.
I wondered for a moment if he were lying, dead,
At the bottom of one of these heaps,
But immediately denied the thought.
'My husband will come back alive to Uchikoshi!' I vowed.
'Look,' I reasoned,
'Even women and children like us could survive this disaster.
He was a man, an armed soldier.
He must have been evacuated somewhere.
He must be safe and sound.'

At that point, I began to worry more about you children.
I had left you behind on the sandbank.
So I quit looking for your Dad,
And decided to return to you.

Nam'amidabutsu.
Nam'amidabutsu.

May the souls of those poor people rest in peace.

Scorched Ruins

August 7, 1945

Photo by Mitsugi Kishida

Photo by Satsuo Nakata

Devastated Cityscape

August 12, 1945

Photo by Shigeo Hayashi

A burned-out streetcar

Photo by Yotsugi Kawahara

Hiroshima Prefectural Industry Promotion Hall
(A-bomb Dome)

November 1945

(About three months after the bombing)

Photo by US Army

Soon after the bombing, this river was packed with thousands of floating corpses.

Burn Victims

August 7, 1945

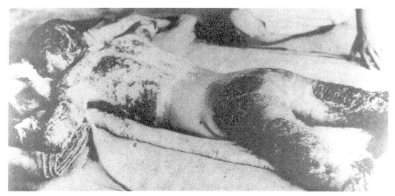

Photo by Masami Onuka

Photo by Masami Onuka

Both men were directly exposed to the heat rays of the atomic bomb within half of a mile of the hypocenter. It is estimated that approximately 50% of those persons exposed and without cover one mile from the hypocenter died on August 6th, with fatality rates rising to 80 to 100% closer to the hypocenter.

Charred Remains of Soldiers

August 10, 1945

Photo by Satsuo Nakata

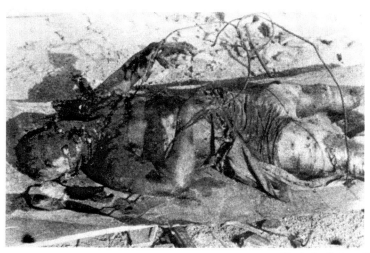

Photo by Satsuo Nakata

Those within the blast zone of the atomic bomb suffered from extreme variations in both heat and pressure. After the initial blast wind swept by, the air pressure momentarily dropped so low that, in the bottom photograph, the dead soldier's eyeballs literally popped out of their sockets.

Schoolgirls with Burns

August 10, 1945

Photo by Hajime Miyatake Asahi Shinbun-sha

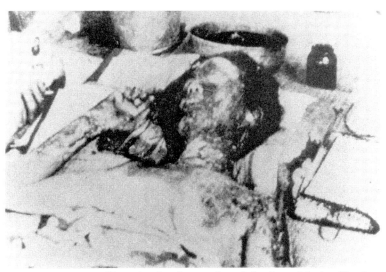

Photo by the photo union of the Army Marine Headquarters

Those who had the misfortune to have faces and limbs exposed to the flash heat sustained terrible injuries.

4. The Remains of Uncle Yataro

The next day,
Taking all three of you children with me,
I decided to visit the ruins of your Grandma's house near Tokaichi,
Less than half a mile west of the hypocenter.
At the time of the bombing,
My brother, Yataro, had been at home.

From the sandbank,
All four of us staggered and stumbled along the streets
Covered by debris and charred rubble.
Some spots were still too hot to step on,
So I held your hands to guide you to a safer place.
But no such place was there.
Dead bodies and skeletons were scattered everywhere.

Amid the blackened rubble of a burned down house,
Two skeletons lay,
One large and another small — hugging each other.

Among the debris of a concrete building,
Several scorched bodies were scattered.
Some of their skulls were crushed, oozing brain . . .

Trying to avoid the debris,
I stepped on a skeleton.

You tripped over a scorched body
That lay like a charred log.

The day before,
I saw five boy students, all badly burned.
They sat in a circle begging for water.
Today,
They were all dead . . .

By this time,
Many people had come out to the scorched plain
Looking for their loved ones.
Some were healthy,
As they came from outside Hiroshima City.
But many were just like us,
With gashes on their heads,
With shards of glass still stuck in their faces,
Or red with burns, and still bleeding,
Dragging their feet, limping and stumbling,
They scoured the places,
Calling the names of their loved ones,
Asking everyone for any clues to their whereabouts.

Breathing was difficult,
As the air was thick with rank, smoky smells,
With the stench of so many decomposing bodies.

Once in a while
Red burned bodies — swollen more than twice their normal size —
Spewed the muddy goo from their mouths and noses . . .
Because some still retained body fluid that had been boiled from
    above and below
By the scorching summer sun
And by the still hot ground where they lay.

As we got closer to the Aioi Bridge,
The burned bodies changed from red to dark brown to black.

Many bodies were half cremated.
Some had burned flesh clinging to their bones.
One had two leg bones sticking out of a scorched body.

A man with a sling made of rags around his neck
Kept on lifting and turning swollen bodies,
Looking for his father.

A brother and a sister, both middle school students,
Injured and burned,
Were collecting ashes of their mother into a twisted pail.
Her last word had been,
"Leave me and flee! Now!"

A man with a blood-soaked bandage around his head,
Carrying his injured mother on his back,
Ran past us.
His mother kept on calling,
"Ritsuko! Where are you?"
"Hurry up! Hurry up and find her!"

Indeed, everyone had to hurry up and find his or her loved ones,
As military trucks came into the city,
And started loading dead bodies into a truck bed.

First, three soldiers tried to lift a burned body,
But they dropped it to the ground, losing their grip,
When its skin sloughed off.

So they called in two more soldiers.
Two stood at each hand, two at each leg, and one at a head of a
    burned body,
And lifted the body, and flung it into the truck.

But soon they realized there were too many corpses.
So they started to use shovels to scoop up the bodies,
And whirled them to the truck bed just like dirt.

When the truck was full,
They drove away,
Leaving a faint whisper,
"Tasukete!"[24]
Coming from amid the pile.

The entire city was reduced to a vast scorched plain
Making it impossible to find where Tokaichi was.

I finally figured out the place
Where your Grandma's big house used to stand.
In her backyard,
She had had a stout air-raid shelter built underground.

By the entrance of that shelter,
I found . . .
The remains of Yataro . . .
Perfectly burned into a skeleton
By the infernos caused by the searing heat rays of the bomb.

---

24   "Help!"

You and Shoichi and Koji, all dirty and injured,
With your faces smeared with dried blood,
Still wearing blood-caked tattered clothes,
Squatted by me,
Staring at your uncle's remains . . .

But your stares were blank.

Surrounded by the destruction and horrendous events beyond your
    comprehension,
All of you were still in shock.

Indeed, all along the way,
You children didn't even utter a word.

We didn't even have a slightest appetite.
I don't remember
Eating anything,
Drinking anything,
For a few days after the bombing.

I planned to go on to look for your Dad after this.
But I changed my mind.
It was too much for you children.
I regretted having taken you with me.
So I decided to go back to the sandbank.

You once said you remembered seeing
A perfect skeleton.

That must have been the remains of Uncle Yataro.

Skeleton of an Atomic Bomb Victim

September 1, 1945

Photo by Bernard Hoffman Time & Life Pictures/*Getty Images*

Near the hypocenter, human skin and organs were literally vaporized by the extremely high heat of the blast, leaving only bones.

5. Human Beings Don't Die Easily

About three days after the bombing,
An emergency relief station with just a tent for a cover was set up
On the site where the Yokogawa Credit Union had formerly stood.

When I arrived there,
And showed a military doctor the gash in my left arm,
He said,
"Listen. Right now we can amputate your arm just below your elbow.
But if you wait too long, we will have to amputate it from your
    shoulder."

'I had three little injured children to care for.
How could I survive with just one arm?'
So I told the doctor that I would need to think about it,
And returned to the sandbank.

As the first-aid station was overwhelmed by the burned and the
    wounded,
Ones who still had arms and legs and could walk like me
Had the lowest priority among the bomb victims.
So nobody came after me to do surgery right away.

Devastated by the thought of losing my left arm,
I resolved to do everything on my own to try to save it.
But all I could do was to wash the gash on my arm with water,
And every day to apply just one coat of mercurochrome disinfecting
    solution from the bottle in my first-aid kit.
But as the bottle was the only medicine I had for treating injuries,
I was forced to use it sparingly.
Day after day, I repeated this treatment.

For a long time, the fingertips of my left hand felt numb,
And I ended up with this big crescent-shaped scar on my arm.
But as you can see,
I managed to save it
Through this course of self-medication.

As for you children,
All three of you had deep cuts on your heads.
Soon after the bombing, when the wounds were fresh,
Blood had spurted from you like a fountain.
Yet at the aid station,
A nurse applied just one brush of mercurochrome to each of your
    gashes,
Before saying, "Next!"
I wonder how all those wounds healed
Without getting any special treatment.
You didn't even suffer from infection
Or get some complication like meningitis.

Perhaps just a week after the bombing,
All four of us walked almost as far as Kabe[25] searching for Dad.
In the suburbs outside Hiroshima City,
Many temples and school grounds had been turned into temporary
    rescue centers.
On the way to Kabe,
We scoured as many of those places as possible in our search.

The many bomb victims were left lying on the ground, untreated.
So many flies — hundreds of them —
Swarmed over those who were too weak to shoo them away,

---

25   About 8.5 miles north-northeast of the sandbank.

And maggots wriggled in and out of their burns and wounds,
Having a feast.
Many victims moaned.
Some cried for help, though feebly.
A schoolgirl kept calling,
"Okaa-san! Tasukete. Okaa-san!"[26]
Though nobody was around her to care for her.
But half of the victims were too weak to say even a word.

The air was filled with the stench of their oozing wounds,
And the rapidly decomposing corpses left there unclaimed.

Because all of the victims were maimed and burned beyond
    recognition,
And covered in black by swarming flies,
We were forced to walk through them, calling Dad's name aloud.

But again we couldn't find him.

Despairing,
I decided to take you back to the Uchikoshi sandbank.
But on the way, it started to rain.
We were still wearing dirty, blood-caked rags
Which we had not changed since the bombing.
The rain soaked us to the skin.
You began to shake,
And grew pale.
Yet all that I could do was to hold your hand with my injured left hand,
And to hold onto the hand of your younger brother Koji with my
    right hand,

---

26   "Mother! Help me. Mother!"

And force you to keep going.
Along the way,
You shook more and more violently,
Your teeth chattering uncontrollably,
And you finally fainted, and fell against me;

'Ah, Kikuko is going to die.'
That's what I thought at that moment.

But you are alive and well now.

And so I am certain that human beings don't die very easily.

6. That's Why You Are Still Alive Today

About two weeks after the bombing,
I decided to go to Rakuraku-en[27] in Itsukaichi
Where your Grandma had a small house and some duplexes
That she rented out.

Under the hot summer sun,
All four of us, dirty and injured,
Plodded along the Sanyo Railway tracks to Rakuraku-en,
Stopping to take a short rest at the Koi Station along the way.
It took us a long, long while.

As we trudged along the rails,
How frequently all three of you children suffered from diarrhea!
Every ten minutes or so,
One after another,
Each of you would have to stop and squat.

When we finally arrived at Rakuraku-en in the evening,
Aunt Takahashi exclaimed,
"You all look so sick. I tell you, you should go to a hospital.
What would you do if other people catch your illness?"
Everyone thought that you might have an infectious disease,
Like dysentery or something.
At that time, nobody knew
That your diarrhea was caused by the radiation from the atomic
    bomb.
This disease is what we later called the "A-bomb syndrome,"[28] isn't it?

---

27   About 7 miles southwest from the hypocenter.
28   Acute disorders caused by radiation, blast, or heat rays of the atomic bomb. In addition to external injuries and burns, they included vomiting and loss of appetite, diarrhea, hair loss,

Consequently,
The local officials sent *daihachi-guruma*,
A large, wooden two-wheeled handcart,
From the Itsukaichi Town Office.
That day a stout middle-aged woman came to get us.
The floor of the cart was lined with a rough straw mat.
All four of us, injured and sick, rode in it,
And sat on this rough surface
All the long way to the infectious disease hospital[29]
In the inner part of Itsukaichi.

Since the hospital was so crowded with burned and injured bomb
    victims,
The patients spilled over to the stairways and the corridors,
And even to the eaves of the hospital outside.
The patients far outnumbered the number of hospital beds.
Some were lucky if they were lying on *futon* mattresses
That they had brought in.
But many were just lying on rough sheets of woven straw,
Or even directly on the floor without any padding.

The only items that made the place look like a hospital
Were the basins of disinfecting solution placed at each end of the
    corridors,
So that the staff and caretakers could wash their hands.

Since the toilets were always crowded with many patients
Who suffered from radiation-induced diarrhea,
I wanted a bedpan for you children.

---

exhaustion, fever, headaches, vomiting blood, blood in urine, blood in stools, stomatitis,
purpura, reduction of leukocytes and erythrocytes.

29   About 3 miles north of Rakuraku-en.

45

Searching,
I found a small piece of galvanized metal, commonly used to roof sheds,
By the side of the road.
By slightly bending the four corners of the sheet with my hands and
    feet,
I made a bedpan for you.
I had a hard time of it, though,
Because the gash in my left arm had not yet healed.

Gradually, it became known
That this diarrhea was not caused by a contagious disease.
So the four of us were discharged from the hospital,
Though it didn't at all mean that we'd gotten well.
By then, food had become so scarce in Japan
That the hospital had not been able to provide much food for any of us.
And so we became very thin and weak.

Step by step, along the Oka-no-shita River,
We trudged back to Rakuraku-en.

After walking an hour,
We found in the river a small island that was connected by a land
    bridge.
We decided to cross the land bridge to the island
And to stop there and have a rest,
And share the two precious rice balls
That the hospital had given us upon our discharge.
This was the only food that the hospital had been able to provide us.
I split the two small rice balls in half,
And each of us nibbled on his or her share,
Little by little, savoring the taste of each grain of rice.

Around that time, I started to believe
That your Dad must have died.

If he were alive,
He would have come to either Uchikoshi or Rakuraku-en.
If he could speak,
He would have asked someone to send us a message.
But alas, I had heard by then
That the soldiers of his unit were doing morning exercises
Out in the open on the Western Drill Ground[30]
On the day they dropped the Bomb.
If that were true,
There would have been no way for him to have survived.

Thus, while eating that little clump of rice,
I felt so forlorn.
My house had burned down.
I had no money at all.
I had no skills to earn a living.
And with these three sick and injured children,
How would I ever manage?

Looking down at the rushing water,
I slipped into thoughts of suicide.

If I'd had only one child,
I'm sure that I would have taken that child in my arms,
And killed the two of us by drowning.

---

30   About 550 yards from the hypocenter.

Even with two children,
I think I could have managed it if I leapt into the river,
Dragging you children with me.

But as I had three children,
You and Koji and eight-year-old Shoichi,
It was just physically impossible to hold all three of you tightly,
Because of the injuries to my arm.

So the moment passed.

And that's the only reason
Why you are still alive today.

7. *"Watashi no Ningyo"*
("My Little Dolly")

I remember it was early October.
After returning to Rakuraku-en from the infectious disease hospital,
I finally came down with a bout of the "A-bomb syndrome."

Your Grandma used one of the rental homes in Rakuraku-en
As a temporary wartime evacuation home in the suburbs.
But her small, three-room house had become crowded
With as many as twelve relatives
Whose houses had all been burned down by the bombing.
At the corner of her small living room,
I asked Aunt Tamura to spread a *futon* mattress on the *tatami* straw
    mat floor,
And I then collapsed onto it in a heap.

By that time, Shoichi's and Koji's health had started to improve,
But only you and I became ill again.
I bet you were the one who had the "A-bomb syndrome" the worst.

You lay down next to me and we shared the *futon* mattress.

My left arm with its deep, throbbing wound had still not healed.
And some of the wounds on the right side of my face and shoulder,
Still had bits of glass in them and had become infected.
By then, most of my hair had fallen out.
And I developed a fever and always felt tired.
Soon, I got so thin and weak
From my injuries and the severe diarrhea
That I couldn't even move a muscle.

I felt very sorry for you, daughter,
Because I couldn't take care of you
Even though you were lying right beside me.
I couldn't give you water, even a little sip.

Lying on my back, staring up at the ceiling,
I wondered, in this impossible situation,
What I could possibly do for you.

And it occurred to me that I could teach you a song.
It was *"Watashi no Ningyo* (My Little Dolly)."
Yes, that was the title.[31]

It went like this:
     "My little dolly —
     She's such a good dolly,
     When I sing to her,
     She goes right to sleep,
     Left all alone, she never, ever cries.
     My little dolly —
     She's such a good dolly."[32]

     My little dolly, she's such a good dolly,
        My 'ittle dolly's … a goo' 'ittle dolly

     When I sing to her, she goes right to sleep,
        'en I thin' chee go sleep

---

31   The original title of this Japanese song is just "Ningyo", 1911.
32   Adapted from translation by June Sumida.

Left all alone, she

      nev-er ev-

            er

                cri-

          e-

    s

     Lef' alon' chee

        ne -

          'er

           e-   'er

And then we cried, you and me.

Routes We Walked

August 1945

□ Sandbank   ⊗ Hypocenter

Sandbank to Yamamoto

Sandbank to near Fuchu

Sandbank to Tokaichi

Sandbank to near Kabe

Sandbank to Rakuraku-en &
   Hospital to Rakuraku-en

2. "Oh! I Can't Continue to Speak of It"

3. *"Nam'amidabutsu"*

4. "The Remains of Uncle Yataro"

5. "Human Beings Don't Die Easily"

6. "That's Why You Are Still Alive
   Today"

My Parents

January 1, 1937 (Seven months after they married)

Father (Nobuichi Furuta), Mother (Masako Furuta)

February 22, 1941 (When my father was
drafted into the Japanese Army)

From left: Masako, Kikuko, Shoichi and Nobuichi
His hair has been cropped as part of the induction process.

My Family

Summer 1944

From left: Shoichi, Koji, Masako and Kikuko

Masako
May 1963 (Eighteen years after the bombing: Age 50)

Two Haiku About Masako

Even my mother, Masako,
who was bed-ridden for so long
lived to see the 21st century

And now in the dim light of winter
my mother is still clinging to
a faint spark of life

On November 30, 2001, Mother passed away.

Part II
My Story

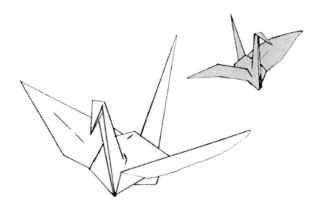

1. Atomic Bomb

BOMB ! This is too small.

BOMB ! This is still too small.

B!O!M!B!

No way !

Not big enough !

The A-bomb was far, far **bigger** than that !

2. Skinning Tomatoes

Please don't skin tomatoes
By plunging them into boiling water,
And then slipping off their skins.

On the day they dropped the Bomb,
Seared by several thousand degrees of flash heat,
Men, women, and children turned to red lumps of raw flesh,
Their skins sloughing from their bodies
Just like how you now skin those tomatoes.

I saw so many people burned just like that,
Their hands held in front of them,
And from each finger tip
The skin like the fingers of a glove slipped down.

On a hot day like that morning,
Please don't skin red tomatoes
By plunging them into boiling water.

3. Anniversary

Every year on August 6, morning,
We put out our father's picture in the center of the *tokonoma*,
Mother sits before us, three children,
We, behind.

At 8:15 a. m.,
At the tolling of the Hiroshima Peace Bell,
Its mournful tone broadcast through the radio,
We sit in silence for one minute.

It is Mother
Who maintains her contemplation
For a minute,
And then more,

Until
Finally, with a quiver,
She turns around.
Her eyes glazed and wet.

Then,
Without speaking,
She stands.

And we return to our morning chores,
Just like a normal morning.
Yet we know that after 8:15,
This will not be an ordinary day.

4. I Believe in God

I am not a Christian, nor am I a Buddhist.
But I know there is a Transcending Power that watches over human
    beings.
I will call it God.

The night before the Atomic Bombing,
My father got an evening pass from his commanding officer,
And briefly dropped by our home.
My mother told me later,
That as he watched our untroubled faces,
He said, "Children sleep so peacefully, don't they?"

We found out later that on the same night,
He also visited his former foster parents
Whom he had not seen for nearly twenty years.

He also dropped in on the home of his eldest brother, Koichi,
And the home of his middle brother, Noboru, who lived just next
    door to us.
In a short night, how could he have visited so many places?

He must have visited us all to say
Good-bye.

God must have told him to do so.

I am certain there is a God.
I believe in God.

5. WHY

When we pass the age of sixty,
It is quite natural to develop some health problems.
So let's stop attributing everything to the Atomic Bomb.

I am a survivor of the Hiroshima Atomic Bomb.
I was injured on my head,
And I had been ill in bed for several months after the bombing,
Suffering from radiation syndrome.

For a long time, I was a sickly child.
I used to catch colds in winter and have stomach problems in summer.
I became infected easily, and the wounds would not heal for months.

Then, about twenty years after the bombing,
I became very healthy.
I lived to celebrate the *kanreki* – the big sixtieth birthday.

The other day, feeling ill,
I went to the doctor's.

The doctor said,
"It's nothing to do with the radiation effects of the bombing."

I felt really, really mad.

WHY

6. No More Radiation

"Let's take some X-ray pictures."
"I don't want to be exposed to any more radiation,
Because I was exposed to so much as a child."

My American doctor looks puzzled, and asks me
"Why?"
"I am a survivor of the Hiroshima Atomic Bomb.
I was only a mile away from the hypocenter."

My doctor looks stunned,
Then, casting his eyes downward, he says,
"I see."

He is searching for words,
Trying to figure out what he should say.

A period of silence . . .

It seems like he cannot come up with the appropriate words.

Then, recovering himself,
He looks at me directly, and says,
"It's just a minimal amount of radiation that we'll use for diagnostic
    purposes,
Equal to the level of radiation that exists naturally in the air."

Well.
"Even so, doctor, I don't want any more radiation."

I still remember how hard I suffered from radiation syndrome
For months after the explosion.
I still have enough radiation accumulated in my body.

Please don't talk about the radiation effects so lightly.

7. Breast Cancer

I developed a cancer in my breast.
No one in my family, Mother, grandmother, aunts,
Has ever had breast cancer.
So I thought I was safe.

Oh well,
I am over sixty years old.
Chances are that an old woman like me will contract a disease or two,
Or breast cancer.

After surgery,
Radiation therapy began.
I lost my appetite, and I felt tired.
Although it was very mild,
It reminded me of the time when I suffered from radiation syndrome.

I wish I could have gone through my cancer treatment
Without undergoing radiation therapy.

Did I have a cancer because
I was bombarded by enormous doses of radiation from the Atomic
    Bomb?

8. Medicine to Prevent Radiation-Induced Cancer

U. S. nuclear facilities may become targets for terrorists,
So they decided to distribute thyroid medicine
To the people who live near the facilities
To prepare for that sort of threat.

If nuclear facilities are destroyed by terrorist attacks,
Radioactive materials will leak out to the surrounding areas.
They will cling to people's thyroids and cause thyroid cancer.
But there is a medicine to prevent it.

Amazing!
There is a pill to avert radiation-induced cancer.
I didn't know that.

But I later found that this medicine is effective
Only against one kind of radiation, Iodine-131, and only for thyroid
    disorders.
It won't work against nuclear weapon grade radioactive fallout.

See?
We can't counter radiation-induced illnesses so easily.

Medicine that works for just one kind of radioactive rays?

Useless !

9. I Will Ask YOU

By thousands of degrees of flash heat,
Your body will be incinerated black, like a lump of coal,
Instantly.

With the tremendous force of the blast of the bomb,
One of your eyeballs will be pushed out of its socket,
Forcing you to catch it in your palm.
A scarlet-stained prize for your reduced gaze.

And many years later,
Suffering from the delayed effect of radiation,
You will die.

It will happen to **YOU**!

And you still continue to develop nuclear weapons?

10. What Would Happen to Our Bodies?

To incinerate a human,
We don't need to reach a temperature of over 7,000 degrees
    Fahrenheit.

To shatter a human,
We don't need to reach a blast force of 1,000 miles per hour.

We don't need such weapons,
That will continue to kill humans with their radiation
For many years after the war.

Yet,
Current nuclear weapons are
Thousands of times more powerful than the *Hiroshima* and
    Nagasaki atomic bombs.

Can you imagine,
What would happen to our bodies,
If we were attacked by such weapons?

11. Nuclear Deterrence

The atomic bombs,
Incinerated us with over 7,000 degrees Fahrenheit of heat.

The atomic bombs,
Killed us with 1,000-mile per hour blasts.

The atomic bombs,
Are still killing us with radiation.

Nuclear weapons,
Should not be used on humans for the third time.

The possession of nuclear weapons,
Will never work as a deterrent to nuclear war.

Everybody in the world should know,
How we were killed by the atomic bombs,
How we are still suffering physically and psychologically
From the aftereffects of radiation.

Awareness of the nuclear holocausts of *Hiroshima* and *Nagasaki,*
Is the only way,
To prevent us from using nuclear weapons again.

12. Don't Repeat the Evil

If nuclear weapons were used for the third time,
Millions of people would die, instantly.
Millions of more people would be injured.
And millions would perish later
From the blast injuries, burns or radiation's aftereffects.

Furthermore,
Vast areas would be contaminated by radioactive fallout.
It would not be restricted to the blast areas.
Yes!
The whole world would be exposed to radiation.

This would happen if some small countries were to use
The mere several dozen or so nuclear weapons in their possession.

The nuclear superpowers still maintain more than twenty thousand
    nuclear weapons.
And they plan to use them on humans,
Again claiming the justification of self-defense,
If they were to be attacked.

Don't you know,
What kind of living hell the atomic bombs created
In *Hiroshima* and *Nagasaki*?

Don't you know,
If we use nuclear weapons again,
That the world would end?

Haven't you learned these lessons yet?

We should never repeat the evil.

13. Looking Back, Moving Forward

I was only five years old when the Atomic Bomb tumbled from the sky.
As I grew,
I thought I would suffer less from the aftereffects of radiation.
I was wrong.
The younger the victims, the more serious the effects.

As I suffered from "A-bomb syndrome" in the months immediately
     following the explosion,
And experienced very bad diarrhea during that time,
I thought that I had flushed out all the radiation from my body.
I was wrong.
Fallout sticks to my bone marrow, and keeps on releasing radiation,
Radiation that will continue to eat away at me,
Even after my death.

My father was drafted into the Army,
And was assigned to the Second Unit of the West in Hiroshima.
And as he likely performed outdoor exercises with his unit,
On the Western Drill Ground,
A mere 550 yards from the hypocenter,
He died instantly (I presume),
Charred by thousands of degrees of flash heat.
But because I was so young,
I felt no sadness at his death.
Oh what a tragedy,
That I have no recollection of my father.

We used to live in Nishinomiya, close to the city of Kobe,
Until the mass air raids over Kobe

Made my mother feel anxious for her three children.
So we went back to Hiroshima, my parents' hometown.
Of course, because my father was stationed there,
We thought it would be better to live close to him.

Returning was difficult,
A wartime trip in a packed train, pressed cheek to jowl,
With passengers spilling out even onto the decks,
Without food for an entire day.

We came back to Hiroshima mere months before the bomb tumbled
    down.
It was as if we had returned just in time for the blast.

Mother said that
I was playing house on the street with my cousin from next door.
I ran back to fetch a spoon — or something —
Then,
    The BOMB !
My cousin died on the street.
My life might have ended at that very moment,
Just at the age of five.

Now I have lived more than sixty years,
And I already have had the big sixty *kanreki* rebirth celebration.

These days, I sometimes wonder.

It is said that radiation alters as it damages the DNA of cell
    chromosomes.
Thanks to the effects of the Atomic Bomb,

The DNA of my chromosomes might have been rearranged for the
    better,
And my cells may never deteriorate with age.

Who knows,
I may live to be the oldest person in the world !

Diagram of A-bomb Energy Released

August 6, 1945

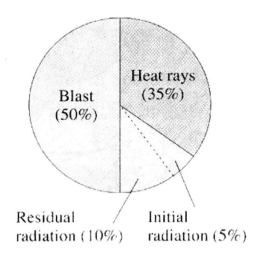

Blast (50%)

Heat rays (35%)

Residual radiation (10%)

Initial radiation (5%)

At the instant of explosion of the atomic bomb, intense heat rays and radiation were released in all directions, and the pressure on the surrounding air created a blast of unimaginable force. Of the energy released, approximately 50 % was in the form of blast or shock wave force, 35 % as heat rays, and 15% as radiation (5% released as initial radiation and 10% as residual radiation). The complex interaction of these three caused enormous damage. The intense heat rays that reached over 7,000 degrees Fahrenheit in the vicinity of the hypocenter, and the blast force of 1,000 miles per hour crushed nearly all buildings, and burned or injured to death many people who were within 1.25 miles of the radius of the hypocenter. Furthermore, the gamma rays, neutron rays and other radiation released by the explosion not only killed the people who had been directly exposed to radiation but also even those who entered the city of Hiroshima days after the explosion. By the end of December 1945, approximately 140,000 people had died because of burns, injuries or radiation.

Black Rain

August 6, 1945

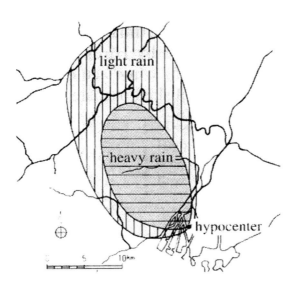

After the explosion of the atomic bomb, fierce firestorms and whirlwinds appeared as the conflagration engulfed the city of Hiroshima. Approximately 20 to 30 minutes after the explosion, black rain fell on the northwestern areas of the city. The raindrops were black because they contained mud and dust stirred up by the explosion, as well as soot from the fires. The black rain was therefore highly radioactive, and contaminated areas far from the hypocenter. Most who drank well water in these areas suffered from diarrhea for three months. Not knowing it was radioactive, some survivors opened their mouths and drank the falling black rain.

Enola Gay

April 10, 2008
(At the Smithsonian National Air and Space Museum)

Kikuko

The B-29 Superfortress *Enola Gay* dropped the world's first atomic bomb on Hiroshima on August 6, 1945.

A-bomb Plugs

April 10, 2004

(At the home of Clay Perkins, the owner of the plugs)

Kikuko holding the A-bomb plugs; the green safety plug in her right hand, and the red arming plug in her left hand.

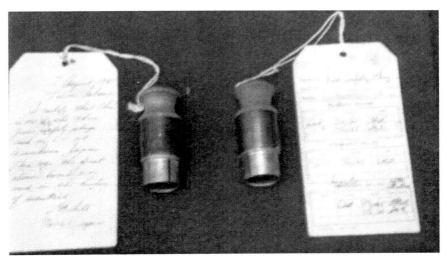

Green safety plug   Red arming plug

Three green safety plugs were installed on the atomic bomb called "Little Boy" before the *Enola Gay* left Tinian Island. During its flight to Hiroshima, Lieutenant Morris "Dick" Jeppson went to the bomb bay and changed out the three green safety plugs for the red plugs that armed the bomb. The green plugs were thus removed from the bomb and preserved. The red plug shown in the photograph was a spare, as the red plugs that actually armed the weapon were destroyed in the explosion. The green plug is one of the three safeties actually placed on "Little Boy."

A-bomb Dome

Before the bombing

After the bombing

The A-bomb Dome was designated as a
UNESCO World Heritage Site in 1996.

August 1978

Kikuko

May 2007

Paper Cranes

Children's Peace Monument

The Children's Peace Monument was built as a memorial for Sadako Sasaki, who died of leukemia ten years after the bombing. Standing atop the monument, a bronze statue of a young girl holds a huge golden crane over her head. This bronze figure is made in the image of Sadako. The monument symbolizes the hope of all children for a peaceful future. Over ten million folded paper cranes are offered each year before this monument.

Cenotaph for the A-bomb Victims

(Official name: Memorial Monument for Hiroshima, City of Peace)

The cenotaph is the main monument to honor and console the souls of deceased victims of the atomic bombing. It stands within the Peace Memorial Park and holds a register of all A-bomb victims who have died since 1945, regardless of nationality. Each year on August 6, the names of victims reported by their friends or families are added to the register. As of August 2011, more than 275,000 names have been registered. The names of my parents, grandmother, seven uncles, six aunts and ten cousins are among them. When I die, my name will also be added.

The Japanese inscription on the front of the chamber reads, "Let all the souls here rest in peace, for we shall not repeat the evil."

With My Friend, Shigeko Sasamori

May 2011
(At the home of Shigeko Sasamori)

Shigeko   *Kikuko*

Shigeko Sasamori was directly exposed to the heat rays of the Hiroshima atomic bomb just over half of a mile from the hypocenter. She miraculously survived but suffered from burns on about one-fourth of her body. She tells her atomic bomb experiences energetically throughout the world. She is also the CEO of the Hiroshima & Nagasaki Peace Projects whose mission is to stimulate an active, worldwide dialogue in order to protect humanity from nuclear harm.

Together with Shigeko, I would like to create a world free of nuclear weapons by telling our atomic bomb experiences.

Epilogue

All of my family members might have died from the Hiroshima atomic bomb. Life and death were separated only by chance. It all depended on where one was at the time of the explosion.

My mother, Masako, was out in the backyard, counting squash flowers. If she had not gone back home to continue doing her laundry only a few minutes before the explosion, she would have been dead from burns.

Koji and I were playing house on the street with our cousin who lived next door. If Koji and I had not run back to the kitchen to fetch a spoon a moment before the explosion, both of us would have been dead just like my cousin who was waiting for us on the street.

Shoichi, who was a second grader, left home for school that morning. His school was located less than half of a mile from the hypocenter. Because an air-raid alarm sounded on his way, he returned home. Soon the alarm had been cleared, but he was a little too lazy to head back to school right away.

My mother, my two brothers and I were just lucky. As we happened to be inside the house at the time of the bombing, we did not suffer from burns, though we sustained multiple injuries caused by our house crashing down. All of us also had the "A-bomb syndrome" afterwards; we suffered from severe diarrhea, fever, extreme fatigue, and infections that seemed never to go away. We were sick through the fall of 1945, but by the end of December of that fateful year, we gradually regained our health.

My mother's left arm was not amputated although she ended up having a crescent shaped scar, about four inches long, just below her left elbow. She also suffered from stab wounds caused by slivers of glass from a kitchen window that had been shattered by the blast of the bomb. Most scars faded with the passage of time, but scars on her right eyebrow, right cheek, and right upper lip were still noticeable through the years, though faintly.

Shoichi's left eye was actually not damaged. But if you look along the left side of his nose, he has vertical scars above and below his eye.

The scars on the heads of Koji and I are luckily not visible because they are covered by hair.

On January 8, 1946, Masako received my father's death certificate, which simply states that Pfc. Nobuichi Furuta was killed by the atomic bomb at 8:30 a.m. on August 6, 1945, on the military grounds in Hiroshima. We still have not found his remains.

Masako who had been just a happy housewife, and had had no skills to earn a living, was suddenly thrown into the world to raise three little children single-handedly after the bombing. As she was good at making children's clothes, she attended a dressmaking school for two years, and became an instructor there. But soon she found out that the dressmaking school was too small to offer any benefits. As her three children got sick very often after the bombing, she desperately wanted to have health insurance. So she asked her husband's former employer, Nomura Securities, Co., Ltd., for help, and she was hired by them, even though it was only as a part-timer. While working for Nomura Securities during the day, she continued to teach evening classes at the dressmaking school. To keep up with high inflation after the war, she taught dressmaking even at home, and sometimes in the homes and businesses of her clients. One such place was Shima Hospital. She taught dressmaking to the nurses of Shima Hospital located exactly on the spot the atomic bomb had exploded! Yes, Shima Hospital was the real hypocenter of the atomic bombing! While working two or three jobs at a time, she also worked at home as a seamstress over the weekends to make ends meet.

My mother learned the hard way that anything could happen in life. And she was convinced that education was the most important thing to prepare children for life. By working day and night over the years, she put all three of her children through college.

Masako started to show early symptoms of Parkinson's disease in her late 60's. She was 78 when she finally told me the atomic bomb experience. Though her movements had slowed down, she remained alert until a few years before death. She passed away on November 30, 2001, from complications of Parkinson's disease. She was 89.

Because of the atomic bomb, Shoichi, Koji and I had a sickly childhood. But after reaching adulthood, all three of us have remained in relatively good health.

Selected Bibliography

Coster-Mullen, John. *ATOM BOMBS. The Top Secret Inside Story of Little Boy and Fat Man.* Wisconsin: 2004.

For Those Who Pray For Peace. Edited by Hiroshima Jogakuin Alumni Association. Translated by Mika Sogawa. Hiroshima: Matsui Printing, Inc., August 6, 2005.

Genbaku Hibakusha wa uttaeru. 2nd edition. Edited by Hiroshima Peace Culture Foundation. Hiroshima: City of Hiroshima, November 1999.

Heiwa o Inoru Hitotachi e. Edited by Hiroshima Jyogakuin Dousou-kai. Hiroshima: Matsui Insatsu Kabushikikaisha, August 6, 2005.

Hersey, John. *Hiroshima.* New York: Vintage Books, A Division of Random House, 1985.

Hiroshima Peace Memorial Museum. Brochure published by Hiroshima Peace Memorial Museum. Hiroshima: City of Hiroshima, 2003. Also available online at www.pcf.city.hiroshima.jp/index_e2.html

Hiroshima Peace Memorial Museum Audio Guide. Transcription of Audio Guide. Prepared by Hiroshima Peace Memorial Museum. Hiroshima: City of Hiroshima, 2002.

Miura, Fumiko. *Pages from the Seasons.* Translated by James Kirkup. Tokyo: Asahi Shuppan-sha, 2002.

The Outline of Atomic Bomb Damage in Hiroshima. Booklet published by Hiroshima Peace Memorial Museum. Hiroshima: City of Hiroshima, March 2002.

Reznikoff, Charles. *By the Well of Living & Seeing; New and Selected Poems, 1918-1973*. Edited with an Introduction by Seamus Cooney. Los Angeles: Black Sparrow Press, 1974.

_____. *Poems 1937-1975*. Edited by Seamus Cooney. Santa Barbara: Black Sparrow Press, 1977.

_____. *Testimony: The United States (1885-1915) Recitative*. Vol 1, Santa Barbara: Black Sparrow Press, 1978.

The Spirit of Hiroshima. Edited by Hiroshima Peace Memorial Museum. Hiroshima: Retaa Puresu, 2002.

Stimson, Henry L. "The Decision to Use the Atomic Bomb" February 1947, in *Treasury of Great Writers*. New Jersey: Wings Books, 1995.

About the Author

Kikuko Otake (maiden name, Furuta) was born in Osaka, Japan. Her family moved to Hiroshima, her parents' hometown, just a few months before the explosion of the atomic bomb there. At the time of the attack, she lived just over a mile away from the hypocenter. She barely escaped death and sustained a wound to her head. She also suffered greatly from the "atomic bomb syndrome." Her father, most of her uncles, and a number of cousins perished during the bombing.

After graduating from Tsuda College in Tokyo, she came to the United States in 1968. She received her M. A. in education from California State University at Los Angeles in 1987. She is now a naturalized U. S. citizen. Based on her mother's account of the atomic bombing, she wrote an autobiographical book, *Amerika e Hiroshima kara (To America from Hiroshima)* in Japanese, and published it in 2003 in Japan. *Masako's Story* is the English adaptation of her original book. She published its first edition through the publisher Ahadada Books in 2007, and this book is the revised second edition.

Kikuko Otake, an award-winning *haiku, tanka* and *senryu* poet, is a retired assistant professor of Japanese language. She lives with her husband in the suburbs of Los Angeles, California.

CPSIA information can be obtained at www.ICGtesting.com
Printed in the USA
LVOW041108020312

271219LV00002B/56/P